THEODORE ROOSEVELT
National Park

impressions

photography by Chuck Haney

FARCOUNTRY
PRESS

FRONT COVER: Theodore Roosevelt National Park preserves and protects the rugged, colorful, broken badlands of western North Dakota.

BACK COVER: Pasque flowers bloom early on the prairie.

TITLE PAGE: The Little Missouri River bisects the North Unit of the park. This river is shallow and freezes in winter.

RIGHT: On a sunny day vibrant colors glow on the hills and coulees of the South Unit of the park.

ISBN: 1-56037-254-0
Photographs © 2003 Chuck Haney
© 2003 Farcountry Press

For more information on our books write: Farcountry Press, P.O. Box 5630, Helena, MT 59604; call (800) 821-3874; or visit www.montanamagazine.com

Created, produced, and designed in the United States.
Printed in China.

Foreword

by Bruce M. Kaye

The colorful badlands of western North Dakota provide the scenic backdrop to Theodore Roosevelt National Park. This land memorializes the twenty-sixth president of the United States for his enduring contributions to the safekeeping and protection of our nation's resources. The park protects and preserves the natural and cultural landscapes that so inspired Theodore Roosevelt. It also projects the spirit of Roosevelt's conservation ethic and his endeavor to provide a lasting legacy for future generations.

When twenty-four-year-old Theodore Roosevelt stepped off the train in the Dakota Territory in September of 1883, he did so with a keen sense of adventure and wonderment. He had journeyed west to shoot a buffalo. TR found the quest exhilarating, with success coming on the thirteenth day. During this first brief visit, Roosevelt became intrigued with the ranching way of life and the "curious, fantastic beauty" of the badlands. Before returning home to New York City, he joined with two others as partners in the Maltese Cross Ranch.

In 1884 Roosevelt returned to the Little Missouri badlands after a political defeat and the personal tragedy of losing his wife and mother on the same day, February 14. TR found his cattle operation doing well, but the activity around the cabin was far too chaotic for his liking. A search for a place that would offer more seclusion and solace led to a site thirty-five miles north of Medora, where Roosevelt established the Elkhorn, his "home-ranch" in the badlands.

The Petrified Forest in the park's South Unit can only be reached by foot or on horseback.

Roosevelt's brief stays in the badlands over the next three years were learning experiences. Here, TR would play out the strenuous life that energized his mind. This land made a profound impression on a young TR. He saw the great herds of wildlife vanish. Animals present upon his arrival would disappear from the face of Earth in a few short decades. He saw productive rangeland depleted due to exploitation. Experiences and perceptions gained here during these formative years were transformed into convictions that became the foundation for the principles displayed when TR assumed the presidency in 1901.

Theodore Roosevelt worked hard to preserve the natural resources of the country. He was able to look beyond the present toward the future. It was his opinion that "keeping for our children's children, as a priceless heritage, all the delicate beauty of the lesser and all the burly majesty of the mightier forms of wildlife" was a necessity.

Theodore Roosevelt's remarkable sense of the natural world is legendary. As president he signed into law five national parks and used the 1906 Antiquities Act to create eighteen national monuments. The U.S. Forest Service was formalized under TR, and 150 national forests were established, totaling 151 million acres. Roosevelt also established the first federal bird reservations and game preserves, later to become wildlife refuges. He showed a deep, personal commitment when he wrote, "In utilizing and conserving the natural resources of the Nation, the one characteristic more essential than any other is foresight."

Soon after the death of Theodore Roosevelt on January 6, 1919, there were proposals to establish a memorial in his honor. Various studies took place across the country that included ideas for national parks, monuments, wildlife refuges, state parks, scenic roads, and statues.

The federal government acquired land in western North Dakota during the "dirty thirties" and earmarked a portion of these holdings for a park. Federal relief programs administered by National Park Service employees were established in the badlands in 1934. Projects accomplished by the Civilian Conservation Corps (CCC), as well as Works Progress Administration (WPA) and Emergency Relief Administration (ERA), included construction of roads, trails, picnic areas, campgrounds, and buildings. This development became the foundation for the eventual national park.

President Harry S. Truman signed the bill that created Theodore Roosevelt National Memorial Park on April 25, 1947. This included lands that roughly make up the South Unit and the Elkhorn Ranch site today. The North Unit was added to the memorial park on June 12, 1948. Additional boundary revisions were made in later years.

A bison's head is covered with thick, wiry hair. Though they generally have poor eyesight, they have excellent hearing and a good sense of smell.

As a memorial park, it was the only one of its kind in the national park system. Eventually, in addition to a connection with a president, the land was recognized for its diverse cultural and natural resources. On November 10, 1978, the area was given national park status. Today, the 70,447-acre Theodore Roosevelt National Park consists of three separate units (South Unit, 46,159 acres; North Unit, 24,070 acres; and Elkhorn Ranch site, 218 acres).

The park is part of both the North Great Plains and the West, blending a rich natural splendor with diverse human history. The Little Missouri River is the central, unifying feature of this wild and broken land. The differences between the North and South Units are both subtle and grand, so each site needs to be discovered on its own. The rugged topography, along with a mix of varied flora, weather, and shifting lighting patterns, provides a setting for a kaleidoscope of colors to greet one's eye. The scene is ever-changing.

ABOVE: A juniper bush sprawls across a park hillside. The juniper in North Dakota's badlands can be up to 200 years old.

FACING PAGE: Over millions of years, natural forces such as rivers have carved the unique topography of North Dakota's badlands.

Theodore Roosevelt National Park is home to a variety of plants and animals. Fifteen inches of precipitation each year nourish grasses and wildflowers. More than five hundred different species of plants, including prairie coneflower and prickly pear cactus, plus juniper, green ash, and cottonwood trees, swath the land. Almost two hundred species of birds have been observed here, including migratory species such as colorful lazuli buntings and year-round resident golden eagles.

Wildlife viewing is popular here. Herds of bison roam both the North and South Units. Elk and wild horses are found in the South Unit while bighorn sheep inhabit the North Unit. Animals found throughout the park include mule and white-tailed deer, pronghorn, prairie dogs, coyotes, and badgers. The prairie rattlesnake is the more famous of several reptiles and amphibians.

Rain and melting snow, wind, and the tireless waters of the Little Missouri River have carved this land, which Theodore Roosevelt described as "grimly pictur-

ABOVE: Prairie smoke blossoms indeed look like tiny pink puffs of smoke.

FACING PAGE: About 60 million years ago, waterways carried eroded sediment eastward from the rising Rocky Mountains and deposited it along the Great Plains. Running water, rain, and wind sculpted these sediments into the bizarre and whimsical formations seen today.

esque." The badlands are still being formed by the interplay of natural forces.

Horizontal earth layers that can be seen in the park are made up of sediments deposited between 55 and 60 million years ago in a swampy region of lakes, ponds, and streams. Over time, the varied deposits were turned into the sandstone, siltstone, and mudstone now exposed to the eye. The presence of plant leaves imprinted in rocks, a large resource of petrified tree stumps, and fossils of freshwater clams, snails, crocodiles, alligators, turtles, and champsosaurs tell of a much different environment in the past. Some decomposed plant material was transformed into lignite coal, and volcanic ash became bentonite clay. Heat generated by burning underground coal baked overlying sediments into a hard, natural red brick known as clinker, locally called "scoria."

In 1978 Congress set aside forty-two percent of the park as the Theodore Roosevelt Wilderness so that backcountry users could face the "savage desolation of the Bad Lands" written about by TR. These wilderness acres (19,410 in the North Unit; 10,510 in the South Unit) offer the chance to challenge all of one's senses and backcountry skills.

Called the "Bad Lands" by early sojourners, this place was a strong magnet to Roosevelt. He explored with voiceful exhilaration, describing it as having a "desolate grim beauty of its own." That same possibility still exists today. The entire park is open to hikers and most of it is open to equestrians.

The compelling story of the park is that it affords individuals the opportunity to enjoy panoramic vistas and a sense of solitude, inspiration, and timelessness similar to Theodore Roosevelt's experiences in the Dakota Territory.

The link between Theodore Roosevelt and the badlands is visible everywhere in Theodore Roosevelt National Park. Roosevelt heartily asserted that interacting with nature would add immeasurably to one's "sum of enjoyment in life." He lobbied to protect resources, firmly believing that nature should be enjoyed in an unspoiled state. The resources to be found in Theodore Roosevelt National Park and the experiences one can gain here are invaluable.

In winter, the colors of Painted Canyon are muted into myriad shades of beige and brown.

Mule deer live on some of the roughest ground in the park. They come to the prairie plateaus to feed and often can be seen foraging along park roads.

LEFT: Prickly pear cactus dots a bluff near Jones Creek. Prickly pear was first discovered by the Lewis and Clark Expedition.

BELOW: The tenacious work of rapidly flowing water is evident throughout the park.

RIGHT: A dusting of fresh snow hides in the crooks and crannies of Wind Canyon.

BELOW: Wild turkey hens look for food in the golden light of early morning.

The 96-mile-long Maah Daah Hey Trail stretches across the rugged and scenic North Dakota badlands. Bikers are only allowed on the parts of the trail outside park boundaries.

Wild horses roam the eastern section of the South Unit.
These rare and special animals are often visible at
Painted Canyon.

ABOVE: Foxtail barley bows in the breeze.

LEFT: Evening light sets this sandstone formation aglow.

ABOVE: Long shadows paint fresh snow at Peaceful Valley Ranch. This ranch was established in the 1880s and is now on the National Register of Historic Places.

FACING PAGE: This snowplow clears a South Unit road for hardy tourists, park employees, and local residents. Winters are often bitterly cold in western North Dakota.

ABOVE: A prairie dog sounds the alarm.

RIGHT: A dazzling double rainbow over Painted Canyon.

Bison were reintroduced to this region in 1956. Today there are 500–700 of these big guys in the park.

This area is referred to as the Cannonball Concretions. Concretions are more resistant to erosion than much of the surrounding rock. Still, even they are not immune to the whims of powerful wind and water.

Twilight tints the foothills of
Theodore Roosevelt National Park.

LEFT: A colorful example of sandstone layering near Medora.

BELOW: Medora, North Dakota is at the park's south entrance. The town was founded in 1883 and named for Medora Von Hoffman, wife of French entrepreneur and Medora founder Marquis De Mores.

Canoeing on the Little Missouri River.

Theodore Roosevelt came to this area to hunt buffalo in
1883. During his trip he purchased a ranch and entered the
cattle business.

Horseshoe Bend in the Little Missouri River is aptly named.

ABOVE: Prickly pear cactus can survive in the dry climate of western North Dakota because it stores water in its stems.

RIGHT: A recent rainstorm has turned the badlands of Painted Canyon a vivid green.

ABOVE: Some sandstone configurations appear like a maze when viewed close-up.

FACING PAGE: Tilting Anvil? Use your imagination to name the many curious sandstone formations in the park.

ABOVE: Mule deer wake up before the sun.

FACING PAGE: Smaller sandstone formations bow
to a big one on the banks of the Little Missouri.

ABOVE: An actor poses as Theodore Roosevelt welcoming visitors to his Maltese Cross Cabin. Believe it or not, this cabin was considered luxurious in its day because it had a shingle roof, cellar, wooden floors, three separate rooms, and a loft.

LEFT: A vista of striated bentonite and ash deposits from Bentonite Clay Overlook in the park's North Unit.

ABOVE: Theodore Roosevelt remarked upon the wild horses of this region, calling them "wild as the antelope." Theodore Roosevelt National Park is one of the few remaining places in the United States where free-roaming wild horses can be observed.

FACING PAGE: Concretions may have any shape, but most are round. More concretions will appear as erosion continues.

In Wind Canyon in the South Unit, gusts continue to sculpt the sandstone.

Look closely to see
mule deer crossing
the Little Missouri.

ABOVE: A full moon rises over banded badlands in the North Unit.

FACING PAGE: Swirls of snow brush a sandstone city in the South Unit.

Elk come out to play in the evening.

Autumn brings even more color to the park.

Twilight during a quiet winter night in the North Unit.

ABOVE: Caprocks look like giant slabs thrust up on a pedestal. Eventually the lower pillar will wear down and become too weak to hold its cap.

RIGHT: Tiny yellow pea flowers announce spring in a park meadow.

LEFT: All that remains of Medora's De Mores
Packing Plant, built in 1883 during the heydays of
cattle ranching.

BELOW: A prairie dog does his best to guard his
home from the massive hooves of grazing bison.

A horseback ride is a great way to explore the park and to see this land
as Theodore Roosevelt did.

ABOVE: Cottonwood trees make it "snow" in summer.

RIGHT: At night, Theodore Roosevelt would light his lantern, sit at his desk, and record his North Dakota hunting and ranching adventures.

Chateau De Mores is now a State Historic Site. The mansion
has twenty-six rooms and was built by the founder of Medora.

There are several well-placed overlooks throughout the park for
viewing the Little Missouri River, canyons, badlands formations,
and wildlife.

A –20-degree day in the South Unit.

RIGHT: The Burning Hills Amphitheater is home to the world-famous Medora Musical. Other concerts are held here, as well.

BELOW: A spectacular Theodore Roosevelt National Park scene: wild horses silhouetted by a luminous sunset.

ABOVE: A coyote roams a badlands ridge.

RIGHT: The view from Wind Canyon Overlook in winter.

LEFT: A cottontail rabbit's camouflage works pretty well, but it's hard to hide those ears.

BELOW: The rising sun penetrates early-morning fog on the Little Missouri.

FACING PAGE: Rain showers have recently darkened the color of these badlands formations.

This bison calf is just a few days old. Chances are his mother is nearby and watching closely.

There are scenic drives in both units of the park. Both drives contain several viewpoints and interpretive signs that explore the history and geology of this remarkable area.

Theodore Roosevelt National Park was officially established on November 10, 1978. The 70,447-acre park memorializes the twenty-sixth president of the United States for his contributions to conservation and protection of America's wonders and resources.

ABOVE: Pale purple coneflowers were used by Plains Indians to treat burns, stings, and snakebites.

RIGHT: A buffalo skull in Shortgrass Prairie creates a scene right out of the legend of the Frontier West.

ABOVE: Theodore Roosevelt National Park preserves a wealth of geologic information that thrills tourists. Scientists study the formations to learn about ancient natural occurrences.

FACING PAGE: Dawn creeps across the Little Missouri River.

ABOVE: Overlooking Medora on a winter eve. Only about 100 people live in this remote town.

LEFT: The sun sets on another still and quiet winter day in the park. North Dakota's lowest recorded temperature is –60 degrees on February 15, 1936. That same year it reached 121 degrees in July.

Even the river sandbars form unique patterns at Theodore Roosevelt.

A lone bison bull enjoys his breakfast. Millions of buffalo lived on the Great Plains in the early part of the nineteenth century. Now these majestic creatures primarily live in small herds within protected areas.

ABOVE: The South Unit awaits warmer weather. The badlands of North Dakota receive about thirty inches of snow a year.

FACING PAGE: Because of its remote location, Theodore Roosevelt is one of the least-visited national parks, but its unique formations and numerous wildlife surprise and awe visitors who come to explore its wonders.

Chuck Haney is a freelance photographer/writer based in Whitefish, Montana, who travels most often in the West and Midwest of the U.S. and Canada. His landscape images, agriculture and outdoor sports photographs/articles have been published in numerous national and regional publications, calendars, and books. In addition, Chuck regularly works on assignment for many of the country's leading publications.

He also photographs sports he passionately enjoys, such as hiking, bicycling, and canoeing. Spending the first twenty years of his life on an Ohio farm gave him a distinct insight and appreciation for the land, so wild landscapes and farm agriculture are two of the many subjects in Chuck's stock files.

For more information and current updates, check his website at www.chuckhaney.com

Chuck and his wife, Diana, and son, Logan, have resided in the beautiful Rocky Mountain setting of Whitefish, Montana, for more than a dozen years.